Name _____

What is a solar system?

A solar system has many parts.
The sun is the center of the solar system.
Planets with their moons go around the sun.

Chunks of rock (meteoroids), big chunks of rock, metal,
and ice (asteroids), and frozen balls of ice, gas, and rock
(comets) go around the sun too.

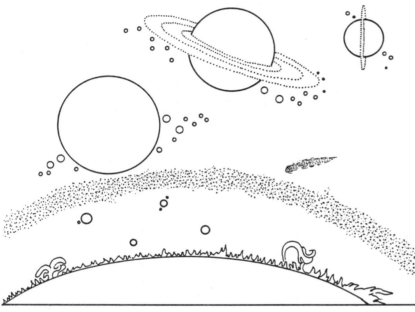

Our solar system is a small
part of a galaxy.
The galaxy is the Milky Way.

Fill in the blanks:

1. The _____ is the center of the solar system.

2. _____ and their moons go around the sun.

3. The Milky Way is a _____ .

4. _____ are big chunks of rock, metal, and ice.

5. _____ are frozen balls of ice, gas, and rock.

Extra: Color the sun yellow.

Name _____

The Planets

There are nine planets in our solar system.
Some are large. Some are small.
Some are close to the sun. Some are very far away.

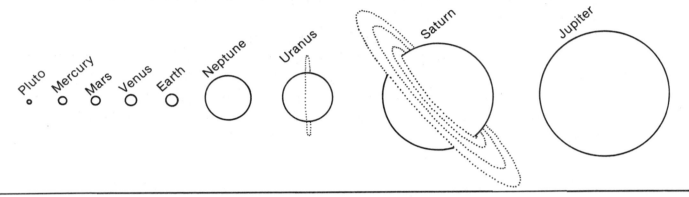

Planets move in two ways.

They move around the
sun. Each planet travels
along its own path (orbit).

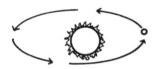

Planets spin around like a top.

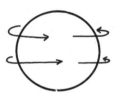

List the planets that are
smaller than Earth.

_____
- - - - - - - - - - - - - - - -
_____
_____
- - - - - - - - - - - - - - - -
_____
_____
- - - - - - - - - - - - - - - -
_____
_____
- - - - - - - - - - - - - - - -
_____

List the planets that are
bigger than Earth.

_____
- - - - - - - - - - - - - - - -
_____
_____
- - - - - - - - - - - - - - - -
_____
_____
- - - - - - - - - - - - - - - -
_____
_____
- - - - - - - - - - - - - - - -
_____

Extra: Put an X on the smallest planet.
Color the biggest planet.

Name _____

Mercury

- the first planet from the sun

- 36 million miles away from the sun

- no moons

Mercury is a small, rocky planet. It is very hot. It has a dusty surface filled with craters (round holes). Mercury looks a lot like Earth's moon.

A year is 88 days long on Mercury. One day on Mercury is as long as 59 days on Earth.

Yes or No?

1. Mercury goes around the sun in 88 days.   _____

2. Mercury has three moons.   _____

3. Mercury is rocky and hot.   _____

4. Mercury looks like Earth.   _____

5. Craters are round holes.   _____

Extra: Find Mercury. Put an X on it.

   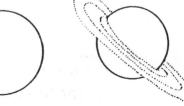

3

Name _____

Venus

- the second planet from the sun
- 67 million miles away from the sun
- no moons

You can find Venus shining in the night sky. Venus is almost as big as Earth. It is a dry, hot planet. It has some tall mountains and deep valleys. It has thick, yellow clouds. Strong winds blow the clouds around.

A year on Venus is 225 days long.
One day is as long as 243 Earth days.

Fill in the blanks:

1. Venus has ⬚⬚⬚⬚ moons.

2. Thick, yellow ⬚⬚⬚⬚⬚ cover Venus.

3. Venus is almost as big as ⬚⬚⬚⬚ .

4. Strong ⬚⬚⬚⬚⬚ blow the clouds around.

5. Venus shines in the ⬚⬚⬚ at ⬚⬚⬚⬚ .

Extra: Find Venus. Put a ring around it.

 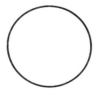 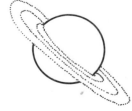

Name _____

Earth

- the third planet from the sun

- 93 million miles from the sun

- one moon

The Earth is a ball of rock almost covered by oceans. It is not too hot and it is not too cold. It is just right for us to live. It is just right for the plants and animals too.

From space Earth looks like a blue ball covered with white clouds. Under the clouds you can see blue oceans and the brown and green land.

A year on Earth is 365 days long.
One day is 24 hours long.

Match:

1. Earth is a ball of rock   is called Earth.

2. The Earth is not too hot   365 days long.

3. Earth is 93 million miles   almost covered by oceans.

4. The third planet from the sun   from the sun.

5. An Earth year is   or too cold.

Extra: Find Earth. make a box around it.

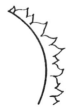   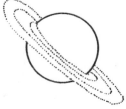

Name _____

Mars

- the fourth planet from the sun
- 141 million miles from the sun
- 2 moons

Mars is a desert except for the ice caps at each end of the planet. It has tall mountains and deep canyons. The soil is full of rust. It looks red. Strong winds blow up big storms of the red dust. This makes the sky look pink. The nights are very cold on Mars.

A year on Mars is 687 days long.
One day is 24½ hours long.

Yes or No?

1. There is a lot of water on Mars.

2. Mars is the fourth planet from the sun.

3. Mars looks red.

4. There are wind storms on Mars.

5. The sky on Mars is green.

Extra: Find Mars. Color it red.

   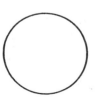 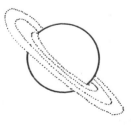

                             THE PLANETS

Name_____

Jupiter

- the fifth planet from the sun

- 483 million miles from the sun

- at least 15 moons

Jupiter is the biggest planet in the solar system. It is a giant ball of gas with a rocky center. No one has ever seen the surface of Jupiter. It is covered by thick clouds. The clouds are yellow, tan, red, orange, and white. Strong winds blow the clouds around. It is freezing cold at the top of the clouds. It is boiling hot at the center of Jupiter. There is a large red spot on Jupiter. Scientists think it is a giant storm.

A year on Jupiter is as long as 12 years on Earth.
One day is almost 10 hours long.

Fill in the blanks:

1. Jupiter is covered by ⬚⬚⬚⬚⬚⬚ .

2. It is ⬚⬚⬚⬚⬚⬚ million miles from the sun.

3. Jupiter is a giant ball of ⬚⬚⬚⬚⬚⬚ with a ⬚⬚⬚⬚⬚⬚ center.

4. Jupiter is the ⬚⬚⬚⬚⬚⬚ planet from the sun.

5. ⬚⬚⬚⬚⬚⬚ is the biggest planet.

Extra: Find Jupiter. Color it.

Name_____

Saturn

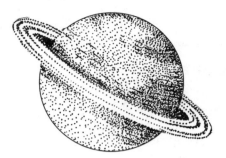

- the sixth planet from the sun
- 885 million miles from the sun
- at least 22 moons

Saturn is a giant ball of colored gas with a rocky center. No one has seen under its cover of haze and clouds. Scientists don't think it has a solid surface.

Saturn has many pretty rings around it. The rings are made out of bits of ice and rock that go around the planet. Saturn is freezing cold at the top of the clouds. It is very hot at its center.

A year on Saturn is as long as 30 years on Earth.
A day is only 10½ hours long.

Match:

1. The rings are made out of   from the sun.

2. Saturn is 885 million miles   at the center of the planet

3. Saturn has at least   bits of ice and rock.

4. It is very hot   of colored gas.

5. Saturn is a giant ball   22 moons.

Extra: Find Saturn. Trace the rings.

   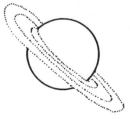

                                       THE PLANETS

Name_____

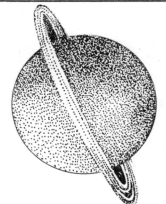

Uranus

- the seventh planet from the sun

- 1 billion 779 million miles from the sun

- 5 large moons and 10 small ones

Uranus is a giant gas ball with a rocky center. It has rings. The rings are thin and dark. Uranus looks blue-green. A thick haze covers the planet.

Uranus tilts over on its side. It moves around the sun like a rolling ball.　—⚪— Uranus　　⚪ Earth

One year on Uranus is as long as 84 years on Earth.
One day is 16 hours long.

Yes or No?　　　　　　　　　　　_____

1. Uranus looks like Earth.　　　_____

　　　　　　　　　　　　　　　　　_____

2. It is 79 million miles from the sun._____

　　　　　　　　　　　　　　　　　_____

3. Uranus has rings around it.　　_____

　　　　　　　　　　　　　　　　　_____

4. The rings are red and orange.　_____

　　　　　　　　　　　　　　　　　_____

5. Uranus tilts over on its side.　_____

Extra: Find Uranus. Put a black ring around it.

   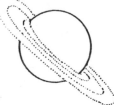

THE PLANETS

Name_____

Which is the last planet?

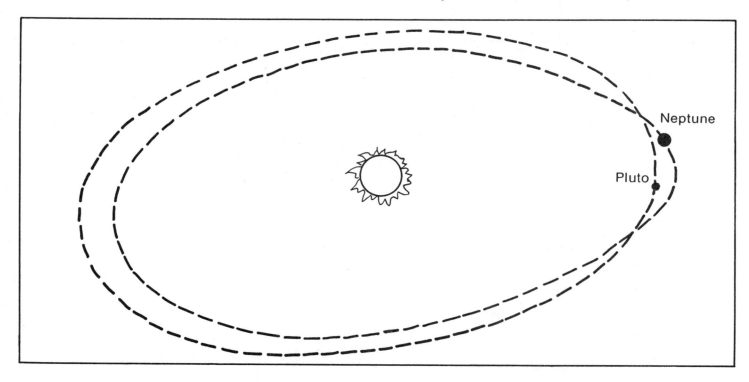

Right now Neptune is the last planet in the solar system. This is not how it is all of the time.

For most of its orbit, Pluto is the last planet. Every 228 years, Pluto's orbit moves inside of Neptune's orbit. When this happens Pluto is closer to the sun than Neptune. In 1979 this happened. In about 20 years, Pluto will become the farthest planet again.

Trace Pluto's orbit with red.
Trace Neptune's orbit with blue.

Name _____

Neptune   # Pluto

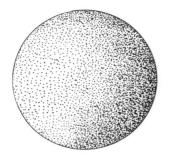

|
|---|
| • 2 billion 780 million miles from the sun |
| • at least 2 moons |

|
|---|
| • 3 billion 658 million miles from the sun |
| • 1 moon |

Neptune is a large ball of gas with a center of rock and iron. It looks greenish. The planet is covered with clouds. It is very cold. A year is as long as 164 years on Earth. One day is about 17 hours long.

Pluto is the smallest planet. It is the coldest spot in the solar system. A year on Pluto is as long as 250 years on Earth. A day is as long as 6 days on Earth.

We can't tell much about Neptune and Pluto until scientists have more powerful telescopes or a robot spacecraft can get closer to the planets.

Match:

coldest spot in the solar system

at least 2 moons

Neptune	- - - - - - - a day is 17 hours long

smallest planet

a large ball of gas

Pluto

1 moon

Extra: Find Neptune. Put an X on it.
         Find Pluto. Put a box around it.

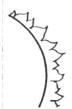   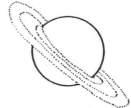

Across The Solar System

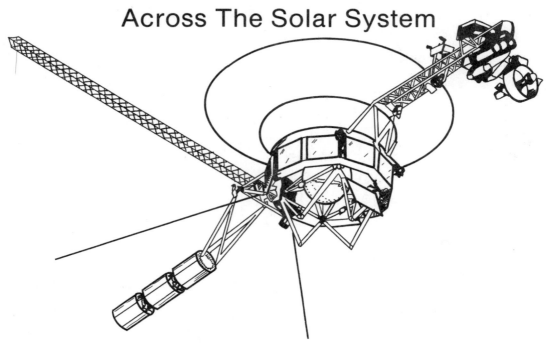

In 1977 some special spaceships left Earth. Voyager 1 and Voyager 2 were sent into space to get information about the far-off planets. Scientists learned many new facts about the planets by studying the messages and pictures sent back to Earth.

Since that time many other probes have been sent into space. Some have traveled across the solar system. Some have been sent to one planet to do a special job.

Fill in the blanks: _____

1. Voyager 1 and Voyager 2 were _____.

2. They left Earth in _____.

3. They sent back _____ and _____ about the planets.

4. _____ study the information that is sent back by these probes.

5. Many other _____ have been sent into space.

Name_____

Find the mystery place.

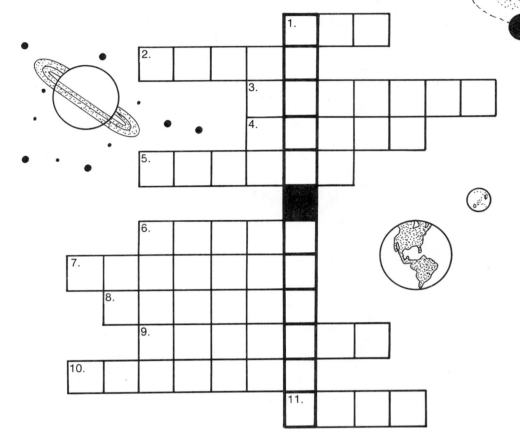

Word Box

Earth
Jupiter
Mars
Mercury
Neptune
Planets
Pluto
Saturn
Sun
Uranus
Venus

1. All the planets go around the _____.

2. The smallest planet is _____.

3. Earth, Pluto, and Mars are all _____.

4. We live on the planet _____.

5. The planet with the most rings is _____.

6. The second planet from the sun is _____.

7. The planet closest to the sun is _____.

8. The planet that tilts over on its side is _____.

9. The largest planet is _____.

10. A large, cold planet 2 billion, 780 million miles from the sun is _____.

11. The planet that looks red is _____.

Write the mystery place here.

Teacher: Sizes do not represent accurate relationships between the planets.
Children will need a 12″ x 18″ sheet of construction paper cut in half the long way.

1. Paste the 2 pieces together.
2. Draw the sun at one end.
3. Color, cut out, and paste the planets in order from the sun.

Pluto

Mars

Mercury

Saturn

Uranus

Neptune

Jupiter

Earth

Venus

13   THE PLANETS

Find The Hidden Words

Planets

```
p  v  e  n  u  s  k  y  u
l  i  v  e  a  r  t  h  r
u  j  u  p  i  t  e  r  a
t  s  a  t  u  r  n  o  n
o  u  t  u  m  a  r  s  u
p  l  a  n  e  t  s  i  s
h  a  m  e  r  c  u  r  y
```

Earth
Jupiter
Mars
Mercury
Neptune
Planets
Pluto
Saturn
Uranus
Venus

Out In Space

```
c  v  o  y  a  g  e  r  g
o  u  r  s  p  a  c  e  a
m  o  b  u  m  o  o  n  l
e  r  i  n  g  a  x  j  a
t  o  t  o  p  x  p  z  x
u  m  i  l  k  y  w  a  y
m  a  s  t  e  r  o  i  d
```

asteroid
comet
galaxy
Milky Way
moon
orbit
ring
space
sun
Voyager

Extra: Write the names of the planets in order from the sun.

1. _____   6. _____

2. _____   7. _____

3. _____   8. _____

4. _____   9. _____

5. _____

Run the cards on tag. Color with felt pens. Laminate or cover with clear contact paper. Cut the cards apart.

Space Concentration

1. Turn the cards upside down.

2. First player turns two cards up. if they match, the player keeps the cards and gets another turn.

3. If the cards don't match they are turned over and the next player gets a turn.

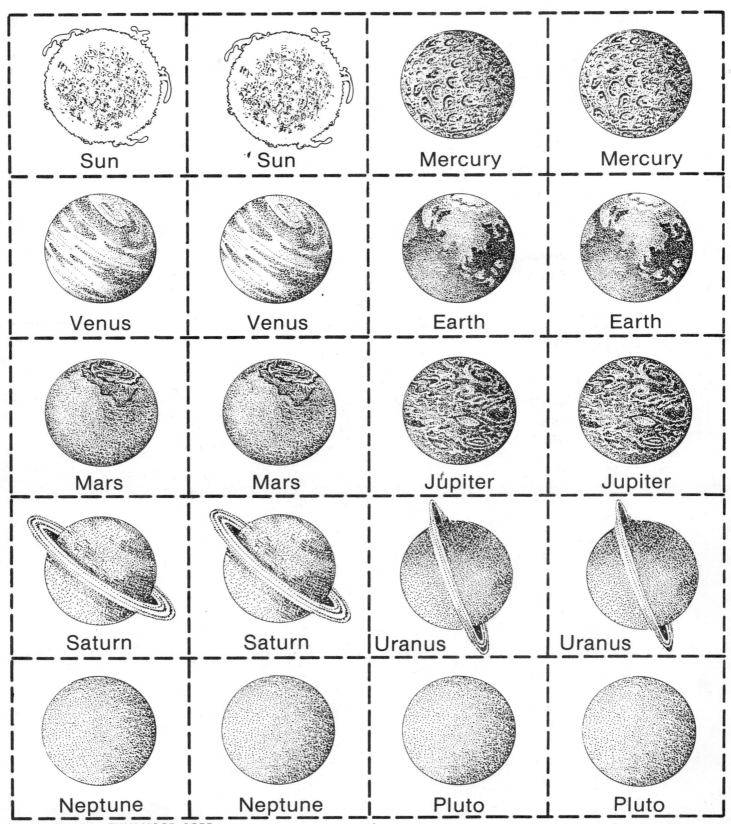

Sun	Sun	Mercury	Mercury
Venus	Venus	Earth	Earth
Mars	Mars	Jupiter	Jupiter
Saturn	Saturn	Uranus	Uranus
Neptune	Neptune	Pluto	Pluto

 THE PLANETS